IN THE NAME OF PEACE

✦

The Way to World Peace

Uzeir Huskic

iUniverse, Inc.
New York   Bloomington

IN THE NAME OF PEACE

The Way to World Peace

iUniverse books may be ordered through booksellers or by contacting:

iUniverse
1663 Liberty Drive
Bloomington, IN 47403
www.iuniverse.com
1-800-Authors (1-800-288-4677)

ISBN: 978-0-595-51614-8 (pbk)
ISBN: 978-0-595-51288-1 (cloth)
ISBN: 978-0-595-61964-1 (ebk)

Printed in the United States of America

To all the peacemakers and peacekeepers of the world.

Contents

Introduction

"Worst thing that can happen is a war, my son," my mother often used to tell me, many years ago. I was about ten years old when, for the first time, I began to understand what my mother was trying to tell me. That was about five years after the end of World War II, when I was living in central Bosnia with my parents, brothers, and sister.

"During the war, I was carrying you as a baby, running from bullets and bombs with your brothers and sister. Houses were burning, and the dead and wounded were lying on the streets. It was horror. It was hell."

When I asked her one time why they were doing that, she stopped talking. Puzzled and quietly, like to herself, she replied, "I don't know, my son. They must have been out of their minds."

Thinking about that later on, I could see that my mother and most other uninformed people, then and now, do not know *why* wars are happening; they only know *that* they are happening. I do agree with my mother's observation that whoever starts or causes a war must be out of their minds.

Growing up in postwar Bosnia with the generation affected by World War II was difficult and unpleasant. Some friends and neighbors had lost fathers or older brothers in the war. Some of those lost were war heroes, and some of them were war criminals. Some friends from school were war orphans, they did not know their families. Food was rationed. We wore donated clothing and footwear. Our common forms of play were war games or soccer using balls made from rags. From those days on I have been trying to understand the causes and purposes of wars. How and why do wars start? How can we see the symptoms, and how can we prevent them?

Between the Second World War and now, many wars have been fought, many lives ended. These conflicts span from the Korean, Vietnam, and First

Gulf wars to more recent ones like the Bosnian war, the wars in Rwanda, Kosovo, Chechnya, Afghanistan, and Iraq, and everlasting Middle East conflict. We have had all kinds of wars, wars between powerful countries, wars involving both powerful and small countries, fighting amongst small countries, and even wars within countries. We will never forget the killing of about three thousand innocent people by terrorist attacks in New York and Washington DC on September 11, 2001. Since then we have had war on terror.

So many wars have happened, so many soldiers and innocent people have lost their lives, so many hopes and dreams shattered. So much destruction and waste has occurred. Why does it have to be like this? Can we do something about this?

This book is about the absurdity of war and how each of us can contribute and take steps to attaining lasting peace on Earth. To achieve lasting peace on Earth should be a moral, spiritual, and common sense challenge to each of us. All of humanity needs to work on stopping wars and preventing new wars from starting. We need to stop mass killings of soldiers and innocent people. We need to stop the destruction and stop wasting energy and resources on arms and instead use that energy to eliminate hunger, poverty, diseases, and many other problems facing humanity. Humanity needs to be prepared for climate changes, earthquakes, tsunamis, hurricanes, pandemics, and other perils of our planet. We need to overcome the need for wars to resolve international and intra-country issues if we want to survive. We need to overcome our instinct for violence and stop mass killings if we want to have lasting peace.

Until the age of twenty-one, I lived in Travnik, central Bosnia, in former Yugoslavia. At that time Croats (Catholics), Bosnian Muslims, Serbs (Orthodox), Yugoslavs, atheists, agnostics, communists, and others were all living in the same town, going to the same schools, working and playing together, being friends and lovers, and in many cases forming families. Communist government at that time suppressed divisive nationalistic movements and religions. It was a similar situation in Zagreb, Croatia, where I studied and worked from 1961 to 1968, and probably in many other cites and towns in former Tito's Yugoslavia.

When I left Yugoslavia for Canada in 1968, I, like many others at that time, could not imagine that the beautiful country of Yugoslavia would one day disintegrate into separate states. When communism collapsed in Yugoslavia in1990, the only common thread that was holding some politicians and leaders together collapsed as well. The religious and nationalistic differences agitated by politicians and leaders in the country and abroad caused the disintegration of Yugoslavia.

Unfortunately, the disintegration did not happen peacefully, especially in Bosnia-Herzegovina. The more powerful neighboring republics of Serbia and Croatia brought war to Bosnia. They wanted to divide Bosnia and have "Greater Serbia" and "Greater Croatia." Many citizens of Bosnia-Herzegovina fought and, with the help of the international community, succeeded to maintain a secular, multinational, undivided land in which to live.

The results of the war in Bosnia (from 1992 to 1995) were about 100,000 dead and 2–3 million homeless, including 1.7 million refugees outside Bosnia. Why did that happen? Could that have been avoided? Had they been less indoctrinated by nationalism and religion the politicians and the leaders could have avoid that. Politicians and leaders with vision for the common good of humanity could have avoided that conflict and can prevent any other similar conflicts in the future.

Each year the anniversary of D-Day of World War II—June 6, 1944—is celebrated. D-Day is the day when 1.5 million Allied troops embarked on the invasion of France, which was occupied by Germany—the day when many young lives ended fighting for the freedom of the world. This day should remind us that at any time in the future if one or a few powerful countries get idea to rule the world, the rest of the world will find the strength and ingenuity needed to defeat those who try to subdue them. It should also remind us of the courage shown by many ordinary people volunteering to go to war and risking their lives for a just cause in a just war. At the same time, on the other side, it should remind us that many people went along with a madman and his followers who tried to conquer the world. That day symbolizes the beginning of the end for Nazi Germany and World War II.

Even now the world is far from being peaceful; many wars are happening on our planet in pivotal areas of the world where civilizations clash. This situation should urge each of us to work for peace and save the many innocent people who are being killed daily in these wars. Since September 11, 2001, under the pretense of fighting terrorism, brutal wars drag in Afghanistan and Iraq. We need to achieve lasting peace in this area.

To illustrate the uneasiness of the situation in the Middle East and some other parts of the world, here are a few article titles from the Toronto Star daily newspaper during July and August in 2006. The following titles refer to war in Lebanon, Middle East Crises, and other world news:

- What ever happened to the art of diplomacy?
- MIDDLE EAST IN CRISES; War without end
- Israelis upset with pace of war
- Hezbollah and terrorism are manifestation of deeper political injustices
- Al Qaeda threatens to join war in Mideast

- Iran vows to boost nuclear activities
- Iraq on brink of civil war, U.S. general tells Senate
- Canada's Afghan sacrifice: Deadly day, new questions
- Testing Canada's Afghan resolve
- Anniversary of atomic bombs explosions above Hiroshima and Nagasaki (Aug. 6 & 9) (About 140,000 residents killed)
- Pondering a Cuba without Castro
- Cubans pray for Comandante Fidel

Additionally, here are some more recent article titles from the Toronto Star daily newspaper, taken from the end of 2007 through the middle of 2008:
- Iran enemy No. 1 in U.S.
- Democrats warn Bush on Iran
- Pakistan in turmoil
- Afghanistan prospects beyond our control
- Glimmers of peace in the Mideast
- Death of Bhutto plunges Pakistan into crisis
- Kenya plunges into chaos, riots
- End of era: Fidel Castro's 49 years in power
- Kosovo: Declaring independence
- Turmoil in Tibet; Dalai Lama urges end to unrest
- The Iraq fiasco, five years later
- China gets singed by Olympic fire
- A bloody day in the Gaza Strip
- World facing hunger 'tsunami'
- Israel's anniversary; Still far from peace at 60
- Palestinians remember '60 years of struggle'
- Cyclone buffets Burmese junta
- Thousands dead, trapped after China quake

The world is busy place; major events are constantly happening. Some of these events are horrible wars and conflicts. Every day on TV screens in our living rooms we see horrible, graphic pictures of death and destruction on each side of such conflicts. TV evangelists are predicting that the apocalyptic end of world is starting.

Why it is like that? I ponder the question of why we have wars very often. It does not have to be like that. If we use our minds, hearts, and common sense we can avoid war. All the people of the world need to get together and find a way to achieve lasting peace, to find a way to cure the sickness of war. Our planet Earth is the only home we have.

War is like a disease of humanity, and we should treat it that way. Today, with our countries' interdependence and interconnections, humanity is like one living organism. We should work on creating a healthy and friendly environment rather than suffer the symptoms of wars. If symptoms appear we should collectively act swiftly, but wisely and justly with understanding of others, to find a way to stop the symptoms and prevent the fighting. Conflicts could be resolved easier by offering peaceful, face-saving solutions instead of threats. Humiliated opponents will work on revenge, and that does not lead to lasting peace. Peaceful solutions are beneficial to all.

Lasting peace on Earth can be accomplished by learning from our mistakes and educating ourselves how to shear our planet Earth among ourselves peacefully. We need to use logical, common-sense thinking and to act accordingly toward the goal of lasting peace. By learning to peacefully coexist with each other. By seeing humanity as *us* instead of *us and them*. By putting *humanity* before and above any one nationality or religion. By sharing our wealth and helping each other. By accepting and appreciating our differences and avoiding the causes of conflict.

Those of us who live in democratic countries can ask or demand that our political leaders support peace and avoid wars to the benefit of us all. Our leaders or rulers need to be wise and not to send our sons and daughters to faraway lands to kill and to be killed. Regardless of who each of us are, to which nationality, religion or non-religious group, or political system we belong to, lasting peace on Earth would be beneficial to all of us. Why we do not have it? Why we do not see the importance of lasting peace in the world?

This book explains why we should eliminate and prevent unnecessary wars. It attempts to describe how we can coexist peacefully and the many ways we can devote our energy and intellect to the betterment and future of humanity. What can be done to prevent or stop a war? What can each of us, as ordinary citizens, do in the name of peace? What can politicians and world leaders do toward this goal?

Some would say that the wish to eliminate war is naïve, but we should talk about it and try to do something anyway. When we realize how foolish, inhumane, and costly it is to have wars, then that day we will cease to have them. In short, the purpose of this book is to portray wars as ugly and senseless as they are, while portraying peace as rewarding and sensible as it can be. I hope this book will provoke or stimulate some readers to talk about, write about, and work toward lasting peace on our planet Earth. We have a duty to do that for our children, future generations, and for ourselves.

I have been writing this book off and on for many years, depending on if there was war in world somewhere or if the world was relatively at peace. When the war in Iraq started in 2003 against the international community's recommendation to find diplomatic solution, I felt the need to finish this book and to keep on writing and updating it as long as I can or as long as necessary. We need to find a path to lasting peace in the world. I hope that many others will write and talk about what could be done in the name of peace and about how lasting peace on Earth could be achieved. Many books are written about wars; we need more books about peace.

The majority of people in each and every country just want to live normal lives—to work, raise their families, and simply live in peace. Governments and politicians are the ones who create policies, make friends or foes of neighboring and other countries, and decide about war or peace. Governments and their agents are the representatives and faces of their countries. The rest of the world judges a country by its face. Therefore in democratic countries, where the people elect governments, the people have the responsibility, duty, and opportunity to elect government officials who appreciate and work for peace. The people need to ask—demand—to have peace.

Leaders of countries with any various kinds of governments can easily see that, historically, peaceful solutions are better than wars. We have many examples in history where colonization, occupation, or invasion by a country eventually ended with the invaders paying the price. The invaders often are forced to give up conquered territories under pressure from the peoples of the invaded countries, its own people, and international pressure. These days with worldwide interconnectedness the opinions of people globally are listened to by governments and politicians; therefore, people have the power to lead the world to lasting peace.

The majority of powerful countries in the world are democratic, with governments that are democratically elected. Therefore the people, as voters, have the power to elect governments suitable to their wishes and aspirations. If the people are convinced that peace is better than war and that military spending could be used for better purposes, then the people need to and will elect the government that works for peace. If an overwhelming majority of people demand from a government a peaceful solution, the democratically elected government normally will not support a military solution. We need to change our attitudes toward wars and toward other peoples for everyone's benefit. Government excuses for wars should not be acceptable unless attacked by another country. Governments that stand up for peaceful solutions of conflicts in the world are the right governments for the future.

As human beings with a long history, vast knowledge, and the wisdom of so many religions and philosophies, it is hard to believe that we still continue to kill each other and continue arming ourselves like the killing will last forever. Our future should be in our hands; we should not let a few lead all humanity to disaster. We just need to realize that and take it as our priority and duty for our children—not the children of some of us, but all of us and all humanity.

Recently I saw a television documentary entitled *Warriors of God*. This program related how, in different countries, different religions are working in an organized manner on promoting their views. Some people are trying to change laws and trying to force their views and beliefs on others, and all of this is done in the name of God. Some of these extremists kill innocent people in the name of God. These types of activities spark confrontations and even wars between different groups with differing beliefs within a county and between countries. For the sake of peace for all, the leaders of these groups need to guide their followers to peaceful solutions and the tolerance of others, instead of to conflict and war. They need to be aware that in any war many people will be killed on both sides.

Living with my family in Toronto since 1970 has given me hope for a peaceful future in the world. The city of Toronto, and many other cities in Canada and the United States with people from around the world living in them, gives me hope that lasting peace on Earth can be achieved. Presently we have in Toronto people from possibly every country in the world, representing every religion and belief, every race and nationality, all working and enjoying life in peace and harmony. Some of them live in border-less ethnic communities with stores and restaurants that reflect the flavor and culture of their countries of origin. In some ways cities like this represent a miniature sample of the whole world, living in peace and harmony together. If that is possible here in Toronto, it should be possible on our whole planet Earth.

Uzeir Huskic, May 30, 2008

The reader should keep these two notes in mind while reading this book:
1. In this book the words *we* and *us* are used to mean "the people of the world or of most countries in the world", not to mean just the residents of any particular country.
2. Most of the data and quotations in this book can be found on the Internet or in almanacs, encyclopedias, or the books listed in the references section.

1

Wars, Wars Casualties, and Military Spending

What is a war? To the majority of people today a war is what they have seen on TV, in the movies, or read about in books or newspapers. Some have experienced war themselves firsthand, and to a few a war is an adventure. To most of us a war is the worst thing that can happen. War is a horror and hell.

As per a dictionary, a war is an armed conflict between nations or states, or between different parties in the same state. The following are some realistic descriptions of war situations, which help us to see true, ugly side of war:

- War is when there are indiscriminate bombardments, when enemies are shooting to kill combatants (and sometimes innocent bystanders) and are causing the destruction of buildings and the environment.

- War is when a bombardment of your town, of your house, wakes you and your family in the middle of a cold night, and all of you have to run out of your burning home to safety.

- War is when you and your family, with all your dreams, hopes, and aspirations, are destroyed or your entire town or city is eradicated by an atomic bomb or bombs.

1

- War is when, as described by a Nagasaki survivor after the atomic bomb explosion, "I saw a huddle of half-naked people. Their bodies were puffed up like balloons; their skin was peeling off in strips, hanging down like shreds of rag. They were so still I thought they were dead but they were not; they kept moaning, 'water, give me water'... I would rather blind myself than ever have to see such a thing again."

- War is when your only child is brought back from the front in a faraway land in a coffin.

- War is when you see war pictures on TV or in movies and you add to that sense of cold or heat, the hunger and thirst, the fright, the wounds, hurting, and pain. And you add to that the sense of agony that your son or daughter could possibly be in a similar situation.

- War is when wet, cold, and seasick soldiers are advancing toward the shore under constant fire from the enemy's shorelines.

- War is when occupying enemy forces deprive you, your family, and your neighbors of human dignity and treat you like animals for days or years. It is when you realize that death is better than miserable life and decide to be a terrorist or a suicide bomber.

- War is when you and your country are suffering under occupying forces for years and the rest of the world seems to forgotten you and your country.

- War is when refugees from a war zone cry out, "They killed my husband," "They killed my children," "They burned my house," and, "They took my cattle."

- War is when your government decides to send you or your sons and daughters, for unclear or senseless reasons, to faraway lands to invade them and interfere in their internal matters on the pretense that these lands are a threat to you and your country.

- War is when you as a soldier come to a faraway country with hopes and aspirations of being a liberator of the people, but soon after risking your life you realize that some or most of "liberated" people see you as an invader and enemy.

- War is when your political and military leaders decide on an unjustifiable war knowing that thousands of soldiers and innocent civilians will be killed on both sides of the conflict.

- War is when your brother or friend or you come home from a conflict without an arm or leg or both.

The above are just a few samples to show how ugly a war can be.

Is that what any normal decent human being wants for himself, for his family, for any human being on Earth? Most of us would say no. If so, why we are doing the above things? Why we are letting this happen to anyone on this planet? As it is now, planet Earth is our species' only home. If we have peace at home we have prosperity; if we have peace on Earth we will have prosperity everywhere on the planet. If we have wars we will have destruction and killings.

Unfortunately we have situations when we have a duty and moral obligation to go to or take part in a war. These only situations are when we are acting in defense of our country or on behalf of justice in the world against an aggressor. Many citizens are willing and proud to go to war for national defense, but not to a war in faraway land for unjustifiable reasons. Unfortunately some countries still act aggressively against other countries. In the future when all of us stop being the aggressors, wars will be thing of the past. Let us work on that.

As per recent data from some leading encyclopedias and almanacs we have the following statistics about wars, casualties, and military spending.

Casualties of a few well-known wars :

-   World War I: about 20 million lost lives
-   World War II: about 55 million lost lives and 30 million refugees
-   Vietnam War: almost 60,000 lost American lives, 350,000 American casualties, and 2 million lost Vietnamese lives
-   Afghanistan war: 748 coalition deaths including 475 Americans deaths (17 Jan 2008, CNN)
-   Iraq war: 4,210 coalition deaths including 3,904 American deaths (17 Jan 2008, CNN)

Defense expenditures and active military personnel, as of 2001:

Canada:	US$7,745 million	56.8 thousand persons
United States:	US$322,365 million	1,367.7 thousand persons
World (Total):	US$835,242 million	20,415.7 thousand persons

From these statistics we can see how we have been killing each other and how much we have been spending to do so. These figures do not include the other costs of wars—the cost of destruction due to fighting and the lives lost afterward due to the consequences of wars. The costs of war are enormous.

As of January 2008, the war in Iraq—just Iraq—has reportedly cost the United States about US$2 trillion? Is this what we want to continue doing to ourselves in the future? Is it humane and sensible to fight among ourselves in times when we are so interconnected through TV, the Internet, and other media? We are so intermixed by immigration in many parts of the world, so we know we can tolerate each other and live in peace. Just imagine how many good things could be done in the United States and around the world with that amount of money. How many hungry, sick, and disadvantaged children and adults worldwide could be helped for the cost of one unnecessary war? Besides, from the past and the present we know that there have been many obstacles, perils, and challenges to the human race to overcome to survive on our planet even without fighting among ourselves.

Since we have had the United Nations (UN), the international organization that is directed by the UN Charter "to save succeeding generations from the scourge of war," all countries in the world should be able to resolve disputes through the UN without going to war. It is only needed that all countries, including the most powerful countries in the world, fully and justly support UN agreements and decisions and unselfishly contribute to the UN's strength. That could be achieved if the peoples of all countries demand that their governments work for lasting world peace.

How do wars usually start? We have a few typical cases. We do not need to go too far back in history to find examples.

On August 2, 1990, Iraq, unprovoked and without justifiable reason, invaded its small, oil-rich neighboring country, Kuwait. In a matter of days Kuwait was occupied. International law and the UN Charter were broken. The world was shocked. The United States led the UN Security Council in condemning the invasion of Kuwait and imposing a total economic embargo on Iraq. The United States and international coalition started to build up troops south of Iraq hoping that overwhelming military superiority would bring Saddam Hussein to his senses and withdraw troops from Kuwait. On November 29, 1990, the United Nations endorsed the use of force if Iraqi forces remained in Kuwait by end of January 15, 1991. Saddam Hussein and the Iraqi government chose to stay in Kuwait.

On January 17, 1991, the Gulf War began with a powerful and devastatingly effective allied air offensive against Iraq. In just about forty days, on February 28, 1991, United States President George Bush ordered that offensive operations be suspended and declared that Kuwait was liberated, Iraq's army was defeated, and the coalition's military objectives were met. Some estimates report over 100,000 Iraqi soldiers had died during the war and at least 300,000 were wounded. Approximately 71,000 Iraqis were taken prisoner. Some records claim that the official Pentagon statistics at that time listed 146 United States soldiers killed in action and 467 wounded in action. Combat deaths among allied forces were estimated at about 75 persons. Many thousands of innocent children, women, and men of Iraq died during and after the war as a result of the fighting. These deaths could have been avoided by a peaceful solution of the conflict.

The above example illustrates how wars between countries can start and how governments and leaders of countries can make grave mistakes for themselves and their peoples. Invading Kuwait was unjust and should not have been done. In the name of peace and international law, no country should invade another country. Secondly, when the United Nations approved military action against Iraq if troops were not removed from Kuwait, Saddam Hussein made a grave mistake not to follow the UN order. The aggressor Iraq was defeated. The United States and allied action, approved by the United Nations, succeeded in punishing the aggressor and made that part of the world feel like a safer place.

The action felt justifiable to some, but to many it was not. A peaceful solution would have been better for humanity. Thousands lives could have been saved and the massive destruction of Iraq could have been avoided. The invasion of Kuwait, an unjust war, planted a seed for the Gulf War, a just war, if any war can be justified.

That same year the Soviet Union, the only superpower militarily rivaling the United States, collapsed along with Soviet communism. It seemed for a while that we would have a relatively peaceful period in the world, like the world was heading toward a global democracy lead by the powerful United States. That feeling lasted about ten years until September 11, 2001, but only in regards to wars between countries and not within countries.

With the 1990 collapse of communism in former Yugoslavia, bloody disintegration of the country started. The results were the wars in Bosnia and Croatia. After more than fifty years coexisting peacefully in Bosnia, Croats, Bosnians, and Serbs—at the same time neighbors, friends, and co-workers—started killing each other. That did not start spontaneously; it was agitated and manipulated with scary tactics by a few extremists and politicians. As a result, about one hundred thousand were killed.

Almost at the same time, civil war in Rwanda resulted in a million dead and about three million refugees. How could these things happen? Could they have been avoided or prevented? They could, with a stronger and more effective United Nations.

Wars within countries between different religious, political, or other types of groups can be almost as devastating as wars between countries. It is horrifying to think about what humans can do to each other. Parties and groups within a country need to listen to each other and find peaceful and fair solutions to their disagreements for the benefit of all. We need to learn this and teach our children how to tolerate each other, how peaceful solutions are better, rewarding, and longer lasting than wars. One war often plants a seed for others. If reformed and made more effective, the United Nations should be able to stop these types of wars also.

On September 11, 2001, in the worst terrorist attack in the United States history, hijackers crashed two American passenger airliners into the World Trade Center in New York, destroying both buildings and killing about three thousand innocent people. A third hijacked plane crashed into the Pentagon, and a fourth crashed in western Pennsylvania. People around the world were shocked. How and why could such an attack happen? Who would do such a horrible thing? Who would kill innocent passengers on planes and innocent people in buildings, and by doing so also kill themselves?

United States President George W. Bush blamed Osama bin Laden and the terrorist group Al Qaeda, stationed in Afghanistan and ruled by the Taliban at the time, for the terrorist attacks. President Bush pledged an attack on Afghanistan unless it surrendered bin Laden and other terrorist leaders to American authorities. To this day he warns of a long campaign against terrorism. The Taliban refused to turn bin Laden over to U.S. authorities. The war on terrorism started and continues even now.

On October 7, 2001, the United States and Great Britain launched a series of air attacks against Afghanistan in spite of much of the world's strong opinion against military action. On November 13, 2001, Kabul fell to the Northern Alliance; the Taliban, Al Qaeda, and bin Laden were on the run. In August 2003, NATO forces took command of international peacekeepers in Afghanistan. A new government was formed after elections in October 2004. To this day fighting is still going on in Afghanistan between Afghan and NATO forces on one side against the Taliban insurgency and their supporters on the other.

President Bush in his January 2002 State of the Union address identified Iran, Iraq, and North Korea as an "axis of evil" that threatened the world, even though he offered no evidence that they were involved in the September 11th terrorist attack on the United States. Iraq was also accused of possessing weapons of mass destruction capable of attacking the United States. The United States was getting ready for attack on Iraq. The international community was shocked. For the most part international leaders were against military action, rather in favor of a diplomatic solution.

But on March 19, 2003, the United States, Great Britain, and several smaller nations launched a devastating attack on Iraq, despite pleas from around the world for them not to do just that. In only forty-three days, Iraq was invaded. However, the occupation proved to be unmanageable due to insurgents in several regions. Since then the civil war and war against occupation have been going on in Iraq. Sunni-Shiite and Arab-Kurdish warfare continue there.

The war and occupation created unprecedented humanitarian crises. About 1.2 million Iraqis have been killed and about 4.2 million are displaced. About four thousand American solders have been killed through mid-2008. Does that sound humane? Does that sound like the liberation of Iraq? How could a small country like Iraq on the other side of the globe be a threat to the most powerful country on Earth? Any move Iraq would make against the United States or any other country in the region would be suicidal for Iraq. Iraq learned the lesson from First Gulf War already.

No population of any country likes to see invading troops roaming through their city streets. In Iraq, some of the population supported and worked for the previous government, and they felt defeated when an outside country overthrew their leaders. They see the invaders as enemies, not as liberators or friends. Defeating a dictator does not mean that the whole country will welcome an occupying force and see them as liberators.

An attack, invasion, and occupation of any country by any other country cannot be justified and should never happen. An invasion means a war, and a war means destruction as well as the killing of innocent people and soldiers. If there is no attack or invasion, there is no war and killing. The results of any war are unpredictable. Did we not learn from our bloody history what is good and what is not good for all of us? Peace is good for all of us, not war.

Regardless of the internal situation in a country, other countries should not attack that country with the intention of changing the internal situation in the country for selfish reasons. Peaceful solutions to any situation can and should be found. We need to start doing that before it is too late. In modern times counties are so interconnected and interdependent that any good or wrongdoing of any country to any other country is noticed and analyzed by all nations. Selfish wars and interventions by any superpower in any region of the world polarize the world into blocs. This eventually could lead to wars between blocs.

The most powerful countries in the world would benefit from being genuinely respected, loved, and considered as friendly instead of being hated, feared, and considered as enemies of any country in the world. It would be a greater achievement and it would benefit the common good to transform an enemy into a friend by peaceful means rather than war.

Countries ruled by dictatorships can be exposed and taught through the United Nations by democratic countries about the benefits of democracy. This can be done without threats and interference in their internal maters. We can give them time as needed to evolve in their own way and at their own speed. If a government is unselfish, open, hardworking, and fair toward its citizens, the country's people will see that and will be content with situation. As a result the country would prosper as much as it is possible, regardless of the political or social system in place in the country. Countries need to learn from each other and help each other regardless of the political or social systems they have, instead of forcing each other to change. Transformation from one system to another needs to be and should be peaceful.

Just imagine if President Bush, the leader of the most powerful country in the world had not gone to war in Iraq in March 2003. Imagine if he had instead addressed the world, pointing out and explaining the world's terrorism problem and asking for the world's cooperation to solve it. Stressing that each country, regardless of its internal politics, was needed to help find the solution would have energized the world to work for peace, and the world would have been a better place than it is now after five years of conflict and war in Iraq.

Even now in this situation, or in any similar situation in the future, the president or leader of the most powerful country in the world addressing the global community in a conciliatory manner would galvanize the world against terrorists and in favor of lasting peace and cooperation to solve any future problems on the planet. This would show not weakness, but wisdom of the leader and country. Honest and unselfish leadership of the United States is needed in the world at this time before some other countries are pushed to oppose the arrogant behavior of the United States, as it was after September 11, 2001. Throughout history we have had a few selfish and arrogant superpowers, and they failed to hold and control the world or part of the world forever. It is time to learn to work together with fairness to all and for the betterment of all on the planet.

When we know the horror of wars, the question is why do we still have them? Why do we let wars happen? Wars like the war in Iraq should not happen in the future. They are illegal under international law and the UN Charter. An individual state may go to war only in self-defense following armed attack. All other wars are immoral. How many thousands of innocent civilians will be killed, wounded, or have their lives disrupted in order to satisfy the desires, plans, political status, or egos of relatively few politicians or heads of state that start unjust wars? Wars like the war on Iraq are irrational. Countries that start wars against the UN's approval and approval of many allies can be considered as arrogant and as not acting in accordance with international law. Such wars could create suspicion among allies and create new enemies and terrorists.

The most powerful countries in the world possess stockpiles of armaments, including nuclear arms, in quantities that could annihilate all living beings on

Earth many times over. Any future global war between countries possessing nuclear arms would put humanity at risk of total extinction. Actual possession of nuclear arms implies their potential use; even so, using them would be suicidal. Yet senseless buildup and improvement of effectiveness of armaments continues. Resources are wasted as we continue toward self-destruction. Where are we going and what are we doing to ourselves? The irrational arms race and needless wars must be stopped for the benefit of all.

Wars are the worst things in humanity's history. We consciously and intentionally kill each other on massive scales, killing innocents and destroying each other's countries on our governments' orders for mostly unjust causes. Most if not all of the time, those who started the war realize, at the end, that the war was unnecessary to begin with. Common sense tells us that the killings and distractions arising from past and present wars are all senseless and absurd. The peoples of all countries need to realize that humanity would be better off without war. They need to demand and expect governments to work for the lasting peace of the entire world.

It seems that lasting peace can only be achieved by unselfish and fair cooperation between all countries. The most powerful country or countries should give up imperialistic motives before is too late. They can and should take the lead toward world peace and provide the vision and support to lasting peace with justice and fairness to all. This should be our challenge and duty to humanity.

2

The Reasons for Our Wars

Throughout history human beings have used many reasons to start wars. Tribes fought for territory to hunt and gather food and water. Kings and rulers fought for land to add to their kingdom's sizes. Within countries, slaves, workers, farmers, and the poor have started uprisings and revolutions, fighting for justice, fairness, and dignity. Religious leaders fought or supported wars to spread their religions and beliefs. We have had wars where the rulers of the most powerful countries try to conquer as much of the world as possible. We have had wars where powerful countries colonized other countries and whole continents, as well as wars where colonized or invaded peoples fought for freedom. There have been wars where countries fought for different ideologies. Recently, we have wars against terrorists and the countries that harbor them. In short, major reasons for wars between countries have been to gain territory, natural resources, power, influence, or advantages or superiority over other countries and the world. Wars within countries have been for justice, fairness, human rights, and equality.

We have had many wars. In the past, soldiers mostly killed only other soldiers, but in recent wars, starting with World War I, civilian casualties have increased dramatically. In World War II the devastation of Hiroshima and Nagasaki, with about 140,000 residents killed, were caused by only two of the first atomic bombs, which were primitive compared to the average nuclear bombs existing today. Just imagine the amount of casualties and devastation if we would have World War III, or nuclear war. Are we learning from the

11

past? Are all these wars, these casualties, and this destruction acceptable to all of us? Are they justified and legitimized?

Most of the wars started in the past were ignited by the more powerful or most powerful countries in the region, at that time, in attempts to increase their power, territory, and influence in the world. Rulers and governments were selfishly looking for glory and possible gains by sending their people to kill others, or to be killed by others. Rarely would the majority of people living in the aggressor country gain anything from a war, but many of their sons would be killed in the fighting.

We would have many more wars if humanity had not come up with brilliant idea during World War II to create the United Nations. With the United Nations, we have something more powerful than any one nation, and we have a global forum where major issues facing the international community, including world peace and security, can be discussed.

In spite of international law and the UN Charters, however, we have had many wars since the UN's founding. One reason for this is because the governments and leaders of the most powerful nations do not always fully and unselfishly support UN mandates and resolutions. The world is changing constantly. In different parts of the world, supranational bodies are forming. We have NATO, the European Union, the African Union, the Arab League, the G8 countries, NAFTA, and many other organizations. Some of these organizations are helpful regionally, but some of them divide the world and its peoples into different groups or blocs. We need *unifying* world organizations. We need the United Nations to be fully supported unselfishly by all countries, including all superpowers, and empowered to do the job it was intended to do in the first place—to maintain international peace and security. Or, we need a world government supported by all nations and powerful enough to guarantee peace and security to all nations.

One of the main reasons allowing aggressive war by a country is the vulnerability of the general population of that country to manipulation by its government. Governments, with help of news mass media, can easily change the peoples' minds in favor of a war. If Hitler had not had the support of the German people to start its invasion of Europe, he probably would not have done it. If the United States government had a strong opposition of the people against the war on Iraq, the war probably would not have happened. Common sense should tell us that a country as small as Iraq, which is also on the other side of the globe, could not be an imminent or future threat to the most powerful country in the world. Yet that claim allowed the United States to start the aggression.

Usually a war is started by the government of a powerful country that intends to use the war to gain something at the expense of a much weaker country. That something could be a patch of territory, resources, security, influence in the world, elimination of an undesired government, or numerous other things. It seems that an aggressor, most of the time, overestimates its strength and what will be gained from the war, at the same time seldom estimates properly what will be lost because of the war. Most of the time the aggressor ends up as the overall loser, even in the rare case when they "win" a war.

The people of any would-be aggressor country should question the reasons for the aggression and analyze who will benefit from the aggression. Is the aggression justified, if any aggression can be justified? All wars bring many casualties and much destruction but no benefits to humanity. The young soldiers of the aggressor country will probably kill many innocent people, and many will be killed or wounded. The cost of the aggression will be passed to the people. The only possible benefits will be to armament manufacturers and to some government lobbyists and their clients.

If their sons and daughters might be killed in a war and the cost of the war would be passed to them, why would people support any war where there is no actual threat to the country? The people of a country or of the world should have and use the power to guide their country and the world to peace. They need to be vigilant and not let their governments lead them to any unjust war.

A conflict within a country against government starts when the people or segments of the people are not treated justly, equally, and fairly; where the right to have a normal life is denied, people start rebellions or revolutions against their governments. We have had many conflicts within countries between a government and a segment of people or between different segments of people within a country. Governments need to learn the importance of equality, fairness, and justice for and among all people. Without these, the stability of the country fails.

Wars between neighboring countries can start when rebels from one country are stationed in and supported by a neighboring country are attacked by the rebels' country. We have had conflicts and wars caused by the interference of a country in the internal politics of another country.

The reasons for any war, from past to present-day wars, seem overwhelmingly senseless, counterproductive, and immoral. On the other hand, the reasons for peace are wise and sensible for the present and future of humanity. We need to look for reasons to make peace instead of reasons to make war. Peace is the way to the future.

3

How Can We Prevent Conflicts and Wars?

Why would any country start a war against any other country in this age at the beginning of the twenty-first century when nations are so interconnected and interdependent and when we have gone through so much war, killing, and destruction already? Are we learning anything from our past? Can you imagine how horrible it would be to have World War III with the use of atomic bombs? Or how beautiful and rewarding it would be to have lasting peace between all countries and within all countries? Why don't we all see the importance of lasting peace and work for it?

How can we avoid wars? The following are some suggestions:

1. The simplest way to avoid wars is to not start them. The governments and the peoples of the world, especially the peoples of would-be aggressor countries, need to show strong opposition to any war. We need to elect pro-peace governments instead of pro-war ones. We have the United Nations to sort out disputes without going to a war; our governments need to support that important body.

2. We need to eliminate the reasons for wars within any given country. If injustice, inequality, and lawlessness are eliminated within a country, then most of the reasons for war within that country would be eliminated. The United Nations can help eliminate these civil wars. We

have had many instances where a government in a country is supported by one superpower and rebels are supported by another superpower. This situation creates a perpetual war. The United Nations, who would not take sides, can act as a mediator between the parties to resolve the conflict.

3. We need to eliminate the reasons for wars between countries. We have the United Nations to mediate between the countries before a war erupts. Governments should support the UN for everyone's benefit. The only justifiable reason for fighting a war would be to defend your country against an aggressor or under the UN's command to help defend another country from an aggressor.

4. All countries, as members of the United Nations, need to support and follow the UN Charter and the Universal Declaration of Human Rights. These two documents have the highest rank as political documents in history. Almost all of the nations and peoples of our planet have agreed to them. They provide the framework within which lasting peace on Earth could be achieved. To achieve lasting peace, all we need is for our peoples and our governments—especially the peoples and governments of the most powerful countries—to really *want* lasting peace on Earth. Then all nations will fully support the work and decisions of the United Nations.

5. All countries, as the members of the United Nations, need to support and fulfill all UN agreements, treaties, and resolutions without any exceptions. This would give authority and respect to the United Nations and confidence to all countries in the United Nations to do right thing. These things are needed for lasting peace on Earth. If a country, especially a superpower, starts to disregard international laws and the United Nations, then that country is putting itself above the world community and can be looked at as a threat to world community. That could lead to an arms race and possible war. In such situations, the United Nations would need to proceed with peaceful measures and solve the conflict, also counting on the fact that it would be suicidal for any country to start a war against the United Nations or the entire rest of the world.

6. All countries need to support UN decisions unselfishly, rapidly, and efficiently. That would provide the United Nations with the strength and decisiveness needed to act in the name of peace for the good of the international community. That would make the international community aware of the strength and decisiveness of the United Nations in acting in the name of peace in the world. This strength would discourage any aggression and would encourage disarmament.

7. Countries should have the right to have any internal social and political system that suits them based on their level of cultural development, provided that they, as a UN member, work toward the implementation of the UN Universal Declaration of Human Rights.

8. No country should interfere with internal matters of any other country in any way that could create an internal war.

9. In the name of peace, no country should provoke or offend any other country in any way.

10. No group of people, including mass media or the entertainment industry, should intentionally provoke or offend any other segment of people, locally or internationally, just in the name of freedom of expression. Keeping peace and harmony among people should be more important than using freedom of expression just to provoke. Provocation could trigger conflict and the loss of innocent lives

11. Countries should strive to improve their relationships with other countries and act as members of the world community. They should set the goals that contribute to the peace, harmony, and prosperity of the world community.

12. Religious leaders at all levels, for sake of their followers and humanity, need to preach peace and harmony between all religions and all peoples regardless of their religions and beliefs. Peace is beneficial to all; war hurts all.

13. National leaders need to lead their nations to prosperity, harmony, and peace with others in any situation, and not to a war.

14. Country leaders need to lead their countries to prosperity and to respectful place in the world community without being feared and hated. They must lead to peace and not to wars of aggression.

15. The peoples of all countries need to elect pro-peace governments and demand lasting peace in the world.

All wars currently going on in the world need to be resolved urgently. They need to be resolved from the point of international law and justice and not from point of who has the strength and power. If the governments of all countries, especially the governments of the superpowers, really want peace, they have the United Nations as a tool to achieve it; they need only to use it properly and unselfishly. The peoples of the world, for their own sake, need to demand their governments to do so. Some governments, especially the governments of the superpowers, could feel that they would lose their status and independence by committing fully to the United Nations and their decisions. However, that would be a small price to pay for lasting peace on Earth.

Through recent history we can see that most of wars between countries were unnecessary, yet at the same time caused many lost lives and much destruction. Today in the twenty-first century, with our knowledge, awareness, interdependence, and interconnectedness, wars should be considered an irrational, suicidal lunacy; they should be illegitimatized. For already more than half a century, we have had the United Nations (and other world organizations), which could have prevented many wars if all its members were working and acting with good intentions. Why would any country attack any other country unless she has imperialistic or selfish motives?

During the Cold War, two blocs of nations with different ideologies and each led by superpowers competed to influence and divide the world. This is not the case today and has not been for the last decade. The world needs to seize this opportunity before it is too late, and find common ground on which to build lasting peace in the world. We owe that to ourselves after so much warfare.

We need to choose the leaders and the parties who support, work toward, and look for peace in the world instead of those who look for reasons to start, provoke, or prolong wars. Haven't we learned anything from history? We would be much better off if wars never happened.

Lasting peace can be achieved if the most powerful countries fully support the United Nations. By doing this they would give the United Nations the strength needed to make and keep peace in the world. Countries need to express friendliness and understanding toward all other countries regardless of their political systems. If some political systems in small, underdeveloped countries are not democratic, this does not need to be forcefully changed by another country. The small country needs to be given time to evolve peacefully under the example and education of the United Nations and prosperous countries acting through the United Nations. With this approach will come a smooth transition from one system to a better system without the threat of war. This approach would eliminate or reduce terrorism.

Since most countries are members of the United Nations, the UN Charter and the UN Universal Declaration of Human Rights could be introduced little by little to fledgling governments as they mature and at the end be implemented fully by the United Nations. Diplomacy, patience, and education will bring lasting peace to the world.

Countries are arming themselves because they feel threatened by other countries or because they want to be superior to other countries. A strong and effective United Nations could guarantee to each nation state that they will not be attacked by another country, thereby reducing tension between the countries of the world. That would lead to reduction and possible elimination of arms races and military spending in the future. If we go in this direction, reasoning and common sense tell us that the world will soon be a friendly home to everyone and no longer a place for wars or terrorists.

Lasting peace in the world can be achieved in a relatively short time if we recognize our past mistakes and demand that our governments work in the name of peace to create a harmonious world for all.

4

Can We Choose Between Peace and War?

Yes, we can choose between peace and war. Wherever we are in the world we can contribute to world peace by supporting pro-peace governments and peacefully opposing pro-war governments. To do that we need to be aware of our countries' plans and policies. We need to find ways to influence plans and policies so they comply with our wishes. In this era with our vast knowledge about ourselves, knowing the absurdity and negative consequences of war, who with normal mind would want war? Who would want to kill or be killed? Most of us, living within a community and within a country, just want normal, peaceful lives. We do not think about waging war in our daily lives. If most of us are against war, why do we let war happen?

Unfortunately some governments or rulers decide for our countries and peoples to wage war. The tragedy is that those who plan and make the decisions about a war will be the least affected by that war, and some may even profit from it. Our soldiers—our sons and daughters, sisters and brothers— who will risk their lives in the war will not be asked for their opinions. The people need to peacefully volunteer their opposition to an undesirable war in order to have a chance to avert it.

Since the end of the Cold War we have a unique situation: the most powerful country in the world, the United States, is democratic. The United States and other powerful democratic countries in the world can dictate

21

or influence the spread of world peace if they themselves avoid warfare. People in democratic countries have the power to choose peace by electing governments that are in favor of peaceful solutions to conflicts and by holding peaceful demonstrations against wars. Even in non-democratic countries the governments monitor their peoples' opinions. Any government, democratic or not, would notice strong opposition to a war from people around the world. In that sense we can choose between war and peace. Strong public opinion and peaceful demonstrations, both within a country and around the world, can avert or stop a war easier and simpler than anything else.

We need to talk and write much more about the benefits of peace. We need to demand that our governments and politicians promote peace around the world and lead our countries to peaceful futures. We should praise and celebrate peacemakers similarly to how we praise and celebrate our war heroes. Our children need to learn how to make peace instead of war. We should make and see more movies about peaceful futures and less about future wars. We should not let our countries be aggressors. We need to work on our societies to become peace oriented instead of war oriented. In this way we can choose between peace and war. If most of us are for peace, then our countries should be for peace.

From the past we know that some leaders and governments of stronger countries start wars and aggressive invasions of weaker countries expecting to benefit. That is why Hitler tried to invade Europe and whole world. That is why Iraq invaded Kuwait in 1990. That is why the United States invaded Iraq in 2003. That is why many other wars in the past started. The lessons from the past are that the outcomes of such wars and invasions are unpredictable. They do not bring the expected benefits to the invaders. Unfortunately, people on both sides of wars are killed and suffer the many other consequences of the fighting. Historically we know that no war is beneficial to the general population on any side of a war. That is why the people of any country need to be vigilant and must be against aggression toward any other country at all times. People should not let themselves be manipulated by their governments to support an unjust war. No government should send soldiers to kill or be killed unless they have just reason to do so. Thought one just reason would be to defend one's country from an aggressor, a much weaker country on the other side of the globe cannot be considered a threat or possible aggressor to a much stronger country regardless of what they do within their borders.

War aggressions are illegal, they are immoral, and they are both costly and destructive. In wars our sons and daughters, ours sisters and brothers are killed or they kill others people's sons, daughters, and innocents. We need to demand our governments not to put us in that ugly predicament. We need to choose peace and persuade our governments to choose peace for a better future for all.

People in all countries in the world, especially people in powerful countries, need to realize all the negative facts of wars and all the positive facts of peace. If they do so they will undoubtedly become anti-war and pro-peace and demand peace from their governments.

To achieve lasting peace on Earth should be a challenge to us all. Are we up to the challenge to make the world a better place for our children, for their children, for us all? We should be. We need to be in order to survive.

5

How Can We Avoid Terrorism?

A dictionary defines terrorism as, "unlawful acts of violence committed in an attempt to overthrow a government." However, there is no universal definition of terrorism. Three other sources define it as:

"Terrorism is the use, or threat, of action which is violent, damaging or disrupting, and is intended to influence the government or intimidate the public and is for purpose of advancing a political, religious, or ideological cause." (British government's definition)

"[Terrorism is] premeditated, politically motivated violence perpetrated against noncombatant targets by sub-national groups or clandestine agents, usually intended to influence an audience." (U.S. Department of State)

"[Terrorism is] any act intended to cause death or serious bodily harm to civilians or non-combatants with the purpose of intimidating a population or compelling a government or an international organization to do or abstain from doing any act." (UN panel, March 17, 2005)

There are many other definitions and descriptions of terrorism in different countries and from different points of view of terrorists and their goals. For example, many "terrorist" groups helped to defeat the German invasion of European countries in World War II. These groups were terrorists to the Germans, but to the peoples of the invaded countries they were liberators or freedom fighters.

Today there are many terrorist organizations around the world in different countries with varying causes. As long as we have injustice, inequality, and oppressed peoples, nations, religions, races, and political other groups, there is a possibility to have terrorism, revolts, and wars against oppressors and those who aid oppression. If we eliminate or reduce the reasons for terrorism we will eliminate the terrorism itself. Terrorism is like a symptom of illness in a society; the illness needs to be treated, and then the symptoms will probably disappear.

Countries would not harbor and help those who could be terrorists to a country they are allies with. Transforming an enemy country into an ally would eliminate the terrorists' support and safe harbor from that country.

When we have a peaceful relationship between all countries in accordance with the UN Charter we will not have international terrorism, and when the UN Universal Declaration of Human Rights is implemented in all countries we will not have terrorism within any country. Democracy and democratic western values, or any other values, cannot be enforced and imposed on any society overnight. Time is needed—as long as it takes—for countries to accept and implement different values voluntarily.

Most of the time, by their actions of killing innocent people, terrorists are damaging their causes. Using their lives, energy, intellect, and financial resources to help their groups work peacefully for their causes would be more useful than acts of terrorism. The terrorist attacks on the United States on September 11, 2001, resulted in the killing of three thousand innocent people and the destruction of the World Trade Center in New York. That terrorist action brought upon the world the war on terror, the Afghanistan war, the Iraq war, and as a result great uneasiness and complications in the lives of many innocent people around the world. We keep forgetting that every action will cause reaction. Since the results and consequences of terrorist attacks are unpredictable, they need to be avoided. Instead, peaceful solutions need to be found.

Governments need to learn from the past the importance of eliminating the causes of terrorism, and they need to act without delay. In some cases a dialogue with the terrorists could help find a solution to the conflict. A country that interferes with another country's internal matters can expect attacks from terrorists in those countries. Impartial interference of the United Nations—rather than independent countries—in the internal matters of a country would provoke less, if any, terrorist attacks.

The world is getting smaller in the sense that we communicate globally and we know more about each other on a global scale. The world's population is getting bigger and at the same time more informed and smarter. With this global knowledge, more people witness freedom and can more vocally express their desire to be free from government or foreign oppression. Countries that support oppressive governments can expect terrorist actions by terrorists from the oppressed country.

In short, justice, fairness, and equal rights for all will lead the way to eliminating terrorism within a country. Likewise, friendly cooperation between countries is the way to eliminate international terrorism.

6

The Benefits of Avoiding Conflicts and Wars

When we know the casualties, destruction, and expenditures caused by wars and when we know that most wars are, in respect to aggression, immoral, illegal, and irrational, we can see clearly all the benefits of avoiding wars.

Just imagine a world without war, mass killing, and destruction. Just imagine the feelings of all who have suffered because of war when they realize the possibility that such anguish will never again happen to them or to their children and grandchildren.

It is disturbing to see and hear that some politicians in the most powerful nations on Earth are planning for and expecting to see wars and conflicts for long into future. We need to see politicians and leaders of these nations who have a vision of peace. We need governments to say that we do not need wars and that we will not start them, but we will help the United Nations to stop any aggressor.

Just imagine how much money, destruction, and life could be saved by a peaceful future for the world. How many hungry could be fed? How many disadvantaged, poor, and sick could be helped for the cost of one single war?

Countries all over the world have been spending huge amounts of money on armament—which hopefully will never be used—that could be spent on health care, education, and increased standard of living for their citizens. Fortunately most countries are doing that to protect themselves from aggressors and not to be aggressors themselves. But if the countries felt safe and secure from attacks by other countries, under a worldwide peace agreement or under the United Nations' powerful umbrella, they would reduce their military spending. Confidence in lasting world peace would bring about disarmament and therefore also bring instant prosperity and harmony to the world.

7

Who Are We, and How Are We Different?

Many books have been written about how we were created or how we evolved from primates. About our similarity and diversity and about our minds and bodies. About our history, our wars, and how we have become as we are today. This chapter will talk about who and what we are now and how to go forward in terms of a peaceful coexistence with each other.

Most of us are born into a family. Whoever the family consists of, we are each part of our families and raised by our families. We and our families are part of communities and countries. We don't have any choice into which family, country, nationality, race, or religious background we are born. Therefore, we should not judge or be judged, discriminate or be discriminated against on the basis of these characteristics.

From childhood to adulthood and on we are constantly learning and being exposed to many things, good and bad. Our parents and siblings, our teachers and guides, our surroundings, and our dispositions to everything we are expose to influence us, determining who we will become. We learn about laws. We learn about our surroundings, our countries, different countries, the world, and different peoples in the world. We make choices about our lives, our futures, our friends, our jobs, and our beliefs. Some of us move to other surroundings and other countries for various reasons. This whole process is what makes each of us unique. At the same time, we can be placed in groups based on various similarities.

We live in about two hundred different countries, divided by borders established through history and militarily protected from intrusion by other countries. Most of our borders are established by wars and agreements among countries. Most countries are armed, yet keep competing with each other to see who can have more and deadlier weapons even though some countries have enough weaponry to destroy the whole world already.

The United Nations was formed after World War II "to save succeeding generations from the scourge of war," according to its charter. Almost all countries in the world are members of the United Nations, including all military superpowers of the world. The United Nations has been doing good work in many ways, but unfortunately it has not succeeded in fulfilling its objective of eliminating that scourge. The United Nations can be as effective and strong as its members want it to be, especially the permanent members of the Security Council of the United Nations, which are the most powerful countries in the world: China, France, Russia, the United Kingdom, and the United States. It is up to the peoples of UN member countries to demand their governments to support the United Nations in doing the job it is supposed to do.

In spite of our separation into many countries by our military guardians and governments, the people of Earth are well interconnected electronically and intermixed by immigration and visits to foreign places. Most of us are familiar with each other as people. We, as individuals, would never start wars against each other unless our governments dictated war. Our global economy has recently become a borderless economy among many countries. We depend on each other economically and in many other ways. Any war between countries is counterproductive.

Different people have many religions and beliefs, and many of us take them very personally. Most of us did not choose our religions; we were born into them. Belonging to a religion is like belonging to a family or to a nation, and some take any opposition or attack on their religion very personally. Some of us would go to war and die for our religious beliefs. Most religions preach love and harmony between humans, but unfortunately each of them insists on being only right one and the only way to salvation. The result is that throughout history and even today many are killed and tortured in the name of religion, though at the same time most religions preach love and tolerance. What a paradox!

Common sense tells us that not all religions can be right. If so many of us believe in one god, why do we have so many religions? The way to future peace between religions and other beliefs is that religious and other leaders, instead of preaching confrontation and provocation with others, should preach tolerance and understanding of others. The classifications of *us* and *them* need to be avoided for the benefit of everyone, as well.

Many of us are more concerned about a life after death than about life itself. If we do not learn to accept and tolerate differences in our beliefs and opinions, these differences will continue to be the biggest reason for our conflicts. Let us live our lives in harmony and enjoy our diversity without negatively interfering with each other's beliefs. Why can't each of us believe whatever we want and let others believe whatever they want? Let it be a personal choice to be or not to be part of or a supporter of any religion or belief without creating enemies.

Most likely no single religion or belief will prevail and lead us to unified, lasting peace in the near future. Therefore we need to strive for peace beyond and above our beliefs, our political and social systems, and other our differences. We need not only idealists to strive for peace, we need everyone to work for lasting peace in the world. We need an international common sense peace movement and to avoid creating opposition and enemies while promoting peace.

We are divided and different in many ways by living on different continents, in different climate regions, in different countries, provinces, and towns, and in different neighborhoods and families. We speak and write different languages, we have different religions and beliefs, and our standards of living are different. We have had different political and social governments and systems. We like and do different things. Unfortunately some of these differences have caused us wars throughout history. But all these differences do not need to be reasons for wars and confrontations. They do not define who we are. This could be proven if we all could live in a common environment.

People come from all over the world, with all kinds of differences, to Canada, the United States, Australia, New Zealand, or other places, and there they build new nations. These people and their children become Canadians, Americans, or whatever other nationality they choose to. All the differences become irrelevant with the passing of time. Some of us see our old countries, where we came from, as enemies to our new country because of the constant changes going on in the world. A war in any corner of the world will have some people in Canada and the United States be torn apart by seeing their places of origin ravaged by war. They may see on TV that their friends and relatives are being killed. War is ugly, so how come we still let it happen? Even most animals do not kill members of their own species like we do.

Even with all our differences, we have many similarities. We all have similar blood running through our veins. We all feel pain, thirst, hunger, joy, love, hate, justice, and other feelings in our bodies and minds. We need air, water, food, and similar environments to survive. We have similar wishes and desires. In short, we are all human. In peace among ourselves we can live and prosper better.

If we would take newborn children from different countries and continents and raise them together without them knowing where they came from, as teens or adults they would be like brothers and sisters. They would not feel that they belong to any nationality, race, or religion; they would feel only like humans. Based on this assumption, for better or worse, most of them would develop based on their surroundings. In reality they would have originated from different groups, some of which may have been fighting each other for decades. Yet not knowing that, these people would get along, as human beings. Many war orphans in orphanages in many countries after World War II faced a similar situation. This realization of the basic nature of humanity adds to the irrationality of fighting wars.

Only the lack of knowledge and education and a selfish, "me and my nation or religion come first" attitudes are putting us in situations of war and conflict. We need to learn that sharing the planet Earth and its resources is better than fighting and killing each other for them. We all live on and share the planet Earth, our only home. We need to learn how to share it peacefully and wisely for our own sake. We need to teach our children the benefits of peace and the ugliness of war. Recently we are coming to the realization that our planet is fragile and that we are doing damage by polluting our common air, water, and soil. A world in peace and without fear of wars could easier find solutions to this present challenge as well as future perils to our planet.

We are human beings with all the good and bad characteristics of humanity. We have been able to do good and bad things. Above all we are capable of learning what is good and bad for us. Mass killing and destruction are not moral and good for humanity, regardless of who is doing it and for what reason. Throughout history, most fundamental changes in societies have come about through the majority of people changing their minds about the issue. We have made illegal various forms of slavery, oppression, torture, and murder that were formerly condoned and legal. Now, before is too late, we need to change our minds about the legitimacy of war. Whoever we are and wherever we are, common sense tells us that any war that brings death and destruction is not beneficial to any of us.

8

What Can We Do about Our Future?

From history we know that superpowers tend to keep expanding themselves and their influence on other countries. Due to that expansion, the increase in global population, and the depletion of resources, a collision of two or more superpowers is inevitable in the future, and that can cause a war. With present military capability any war between superpowers could escalate to nuclear war and the self-destruction of humanity.

Most likely, no single superpower would be able to unify all countries in the world under its umbrella of ideology peacefully. Doing so forcefully would mean World War III and the possible self-destruction of humanity. The only solution is to have an entity more powerful than any superpower. This entity would be a valuable deterrent to any war between any nations. The United Nations is poised to be this entity, but to do so it must be reformed and raised to a level respected by all nations or modified into a new world organization to act as a world government.

At the end of World War II in 1945 the United Nations was established to serve the cause of peace among the nations. The Preamble to the UN Charter starts with the following words: "We the peoples of the United Nations determined to save succeeding generations from the scourge of war, which twice in our lifetime has brought untold sorrow to mankind, and to reaffirm faith in fundamental human rights, in the dignity and worth of the human person, in the equal rights of men and women and of nations large and small...."

It is clear from this that the main purpose of the United Nations is to maintain international peace and security. Just about all countries and peoples of the Earth are members of the United Nations, and they have accepted the UN Charter and the obligations to carry it out. The UN Charter and another document, the Universal Declaration of Human Rights, beautifully and clearly spell out guiding instructions on how the member countries should deal with each other and with their citizens. If all UN members and their governments acted accordingly our world would be much better place than it is now; we would not have wars between countries and within countries. No aggression of one country on another is justified. International law recognizes only two reasons for legitimate war. Legitimate wars are those of defense and those sanctioned by the UN Security Council.

Just imagine if all countries would stick to their agreement with the United Nations, that they would not start any war and would work for peaceful solutions to conflicts in any part of the world with any country in the world regardless of present political or other agenda. With that clout and support the United Nations could resolve any dispute with any country in the world. The nations would stop being afraid of each other, and the United Nations would protect them.

If democratic countries see that something should be done in undemocratic countries they need to suggest their solution openly and without any threat. Dictatorships can be persuaded to political changes if they see no threat. The current wars and political changes in Afghanistan and Iraq are forced and barbaric; they could be achieved with persuasion, which would take longer but would allow the countries to evolve without killings and without creating enemies and terrorists.

Lessons from the Afghanistan and Iraq wars need to be learned. Peaceful solutions to all conflicts need to be found. After five years of United States invasion of Iraq there is no end to the war. Over four thousand Americans and over ninety thousand Iraqi civilians have been killed. Since military solution to the war is not foreseeable in the near future, it seems that a pullout of the American troops combined with a diplomatic solution involving the United Nations are required to bring peace in that critical area of the world.

All wars between countries have been started by the military attack of one country on another country under order of its government. Most wars, if not all, can be considered as errors. They have brought mass killings, destruction, and misery to peoples on both sides of conflict. For some reason at any time in history the most powerful country seemingly cannot resist the temptation to become more powerful or to become the master of the world until either another superpower or the rest of the world stops it. For that reason we need an empowered United Nations to keep us in peace before we destroy ourselves. The United Nations is our hope. The sooner we and our governments realize that, the better.

It is up to all of us to elect pro-peace governments and demand a peaceful future for all. The peoples of the world need to illegitimatize wars, military preparations, and nuclear armaments. With the realization of the irrationality, immorality, and ugliness of war should come our duty to eliminate them.

Just imagine a world without war. Just imagine a world where no country sees any other country as an enemy. Just imagine the world as one country, and within that country we all feel free, we all are equal by law, and we and our children all have the same opportunities in life. That could be our future. That is what our vision of the future should be. We have the power to shape a peaceful future; we can do it and we should do it. After all, it is our future.

9

What Was Said about Peace and War

The following are some samples of what religions, prophets, philosophers, statesmen, scientists, thinkers, and others said about wars and peace.

Thou shalt not kill.
—Bible, Exodus 20:6

Depart from evil and do good; Seek peace and pursue it.
—Bible, Psalms 34:14

Blessed are the peacemakers, for they shall be called the children of God.
—Bible, Matthew 5:9

But if the enemy incline towards peace, you (also) incline toward peace, and trust in Allah: for He is One that hears and knows (all things).
—Qur'an, 8:61

Take no life, which Allah has made sacred, except by way of justice and law: thus does He command you, that you may learn wisdom.
—Qur'an, 6:151

There is no way to peace. Peace is the way.
—A.J. Muste

When peace has been broken anywhere, the peace of all countries everywhere is in danger.
—Franklin D. Roosevelt

If there is light in the soul, there will be beauty in the person.
If there is beauty in the person, there will be harmony in the house.
If there is harmony in the house, there will be order in the nation.
If there is order in the nation, there will be peace in the world."
—Chinese proverb

Enough of blood and tears. Enough.
—Yitzhak Rabin

The best way to destroy an enemy is to make him a friend.
—Abraham Lincoln

In war, whichever side may call itself the victor, there are no winners, but all are losers.
—Neville Chamberlain

We may never be strong enough to be entirely nonviolent in thought, word, and deed. But we must keep nonviolence as our goal and make strong progress toward it. The attainment of freedom, whether for a person, a nation, or a world, must be in exact proportion to the attainment of nonviolence for each.
—Mahatma Gandhi

What difference does it make to the dead, the orphans, and the homeless, whether the mad destruction is wrought under the name of totalitarianism or the holy name of liberty or democracy?
—Mahatma Gandhi

Older men declare war. But it is youth who must fight and die.
—Herbert Hoover

I have seen war. I have seen war on land and sea. I have seen blood running from the wounded. I have seen men coughing out their gassed lungs. I have seen the dead in the mud. I have seen 200 limping, exhausted men come out of line—the survivors of a regiment of 1000 that went forward 48 hours before. I have seen children starving. I have seen the agony of mothers and wives. I hate war.
—Franklin D. Roosevelt

Mankind must put an end to war, or war will put an end to mankind....War will exist until that distant day when the conscientious objector enjoys the same reputation and prestige that the warrior does today.
—John F. Kennedy

I am not only a pacifist but militant pacifist. I am willing to fight for peace. Nothing will end war unless the people themselves refuse to go to war.
—Albert Einstein

The work, my friend, is peace. More than an end to war, we want an end to the beginning of all wars—yes, an end to this brutal, inhuman, and thoroughly impractical method of settling the differences between governments.
—Franklin D. Roosevelt

Peace is a daily, a weekly, a monthly process, gradually changing opinions, slowly eroding old barriers, quietly building new structures.
—John F. Kennedy

Peace cannot be achieved through violence; it can be attained through understanding.
—Albert Einstein

You can't separate peace from freedom because no one can be at peace unless he has his freedom.
—Malcolm X

Nonviolence means avoiding not only external physical violence but also internal violence of spirit. You not only refuse to shoot a man, but you refuse to hate him.
—Martin Luther King Jr.

I like to believe that people in the long run are going to do more to promote peace than governments. Indeed, I think that people want peace so much that one of these days governments had better get out of their way and let them have it.
—Dwight D. Eisenhower

Of all the enemies to public liberty war is, perhaps, the most to be dreaded because it comprises and develops the germ of every other. War is the parent of armies; from these proceed debts and taxes ... known instruments for bringing the many under the domination of the few....
No nation could preserve its freedom in the midst of continual warfare.
—James Madison

A world government with powers adequate to guarantee security is not a remote ideal for the distant future. It is urgent necessity, if our civilization is to survive.
—Albert Einstein

True peace is not merely the absence of tension: it is the presence of justice.
—Martin Luther King Jr.

Imagine there's no countries
It isn't hard to do
Nothing to kill or die for …
No need for greed or hunger
A brotherhood of man
Imagine all the people
Sharing all the world
You may say I'm a dreamer
But I'm not the only one
I hope someday you'll join us
And the world will live as one
—"Imagine," written by John Lennon

10

Peace

If war is a hell, peace is a heaven. Peace is something that most of us long for—for peace within ourselves, peace within family, friends, and neighbors, peace within our country, and peace in the world. Peace is when we forget about the possibility of war. It is a state of justice and harmony. We will have peace in the world when we all realize that military conflicts are not needed to resolve disagreements and issues between or within countries.

Let us imagine that we had a lasting peace agreement between all countries in the world. The peace agreement was brokered and will be enforced by an empowered United Nations that is supported fully and unselfishly by all the countries in the world. In short, imagine we have a guaranteed imaginary lasting peace between all countries in the world as they are now in 2008, with the assumption that military action, including the military might of present superpowers, would be used only if approved by the United Nations and only against a country or countries that break the peace agreement and start a war.

Under the above assumptions each country in the world would start to feel safe from military attacks by any other country. With that feeling the countries would soon realize that increases in military spending are not needed, and soon after that decreases in spending would follow. Small countries planning to obtain or develop atomic bombs for protection would give up on the plans with the realization that an attacker would have the entire rest of the world against them, including countries with atomic bombs already. No country would take a chance to start a war against rest of the world. Current stockpiles of arms in all countries, on disposal to the United Nations, would be a strong deterrent to any individual country to start a war. Military spending all over the world would soon be reduced to spending only on maintenance of the current military, and soon after that would follow a reduction of militaries and spending.

All countries in the world could find better ways to use the money saved by shrinking their militaries. Unfortunately we have many needy people around the world who are still hungry, sick, and disadvantaged and need help to survive. Without the threat of outside attack and interference governments can work on improving the lives of their citizens.

Countries with internal political, religious, national, and other problems could ask the United Nations for help, advice, or mediation to resolve the problems. The UN's involvement would be impartial and without strings attached compared to the involvement of some individual country or bloc of countries. In the latter case the government in need would be supported by one bloc or country, while the needy country's opposition would be supported by some other bloc or country. But with UN aid, there would not be any confrontation between governments due to the outcome of the mediation because the mediation would be done impartially by one international mediator, the United Nations.

Countries without enemies would not need to support international terrorists. International terrorism would decline and soon will be eliminated.

The United Nations would be in the best position to eliminate terrorism within a country by resolving reasons for that terrorism while acting as an impartial mediator. Compare this to a situation where a bloc of countries supports the government and another bloc supports the terrorist faction. In that case, terrorism never ends.

Under world peace, the United Nations would be in a better position to democratically and justly tackle global warming, global pollution, and other environmental issues and perils to our world. It would also be in a better position to help a country struggling to provide its people with health care, food, water, or education.

Lasting peace in the world would bring an end to wars, mass military killing and destruction, and huge military spending. Savings from military spending could be used to reduce poverty, hunger, homelessness, sicknesses, and lack of education in many individual countries and around the world. The world would be a much better place than it is now. We need to work constantly on establishing world peace and a harmonious balance with the rest of the natural world.

This is not something that can't come until far in the future. It is something that could be achieved in the near future. We need it now before it is too late. Fortunately we already have the United Nations in place, which is already doing tremendous work around the world. We probably would have destroyed ourselves by now if we did not have the United Nations. Our governments need to support the United Nations fully and live in accordance with the UN Charter and the Universal Declaration of Human Rights. We need to demand this from our governments. All countries need to contribute to the improvement of the United Nations in order to give us the most effective the United Nations. They need to unite forces to maintain peace and security in the world. This seems to be the most logical and fastest way to achieve lasting peace in the world.

Conclusion

Our future depends on each of us. In democracy each of us is equal and has the privilege to vote. We have the power to elect representatives and leaders that can lead us to the future that we want. We can make demands on our governments to lead us to a peaceful future. In the world's politics and with the existence of the United Nations, the leaders of all countries, including dictators, are monitoring their peoples' opinions and take these opinions into consideration when deciding about taking aggression on other country. If we know that war is detrimental—not beneficial—to all of us, then we need to show that to our governments and demand peace.

It should be our moral and spiritual duty to stop wars, mass killings, destruction, and the waste of energy, time, and resources that could be used in needy areas around the world. Areas like hunger, health, homelessness, medicine, global warming, space exploration, and unforeseen possible future natural disasters or other needs.

It looks like the only way to achieve a peaceful future on our planet is if we and our governments start thinking about people of the world in terms of *we* instead of *us and them*. We need to start respecting each other and stop threatening each other. By doing this each country will start to feel safer within its borders from attacks by neighbors or powerful, faraway countries. Little by little the countries will start to see no threat from each other regardless what political, religious, or social systems they have. When this global feeling is achieved countries will slow down and eventually stop the arms race and start global disarmament. If a country will not cooperate and tries to interfere in the establishment of global lasting peace, the country will have the United Nations or the rest of the world to deal with.

We need to proceed with understanding and gentleness to each other, to each other's beliefs, backgrounds, and histories. We need to avoid provocations, hatred, and threats in order to avoid conflicts and wars.

If we only had one nation, one religion, one political system, and one consistent standard of living across the globe, we probably would not have as many wars as we have had. Since we do not have that, we need to accept each other as we are, and we and our governments all need to support the United Nations, to keep the peace until we learn to be peaceful with each other.

The world as one country is a prospect for the distant future. Before that and much sooner we could have the world as a union of all or almost all the countries in the world. If we use history as a guide, that is the trend we are heading toward. Families became tribes, tribes became states, states became countries, and now countries are uniting in unions or blocs, such as the European Union. Our economies are borderless; regional and global economies are in place already. Next step is the world union.

The European Union is an enormous economic superpower with a gigantic market of over 425 million people in twenty-five countries, with even more countries applying to join. It is amazing to see a union of twenty-five countries with a common currency and a single market, free of barriers to the movement of goods, services, capital, and labor. This is especially amazing because some of these countries were at war with each other just sixty-five years ago. This was achieved democratically and without force or intimidation. This is what all countries in the world need to work on—democratic, peaceful unification.

Unfortunately the world is not yet ready for unification similar to the European Union. It took about fifty years of work to form the European Union, and the work is still in progress. Global unification will need at least that many years. Some of us still need to be convinced that peaceful sharing of the world is better than fighting for pieces of it.

Fortunately we do not need to wait for world unification to have lasting peace in the world. We already have the United Nations, and we need only for all countries to put their full, unselfish, and honest support behind the work and objectives of the United Nations. We the people need to demand that from our governments.

We can see from history's wars how wars are deadly, destructive, immoral, and a step backward in human progress. We need to learn how to prevent wars. All of us need to see that as a real possibility and as a challenge. We need to talk about it, teach our children about it, elect pro-peace officials for our governments, and demand from our governments lasting peace and peaceful solutions to future disagreements and conflicts in the world.

Each of us needs to take a moment, from time to time, and think about how fortunate we are to exist and experience life with all its beauty and challenges on our life-giving and beautiful planet Earth. We only need to eliminate the dark clouds above all of us—the clouds of wars, mass killings, and needless destruction—and proceed in peace and harmony to share and live on our planet Earth, our only home in the vast universe.

Note to the reader

Dear reader,

As you know, the purpose of this book is to embrace lasting world peace and open discussion about how to do so. If you have any comments, suggestions, or ideas regarding the achievement of peace or the extinction of war, please e-mail me at:

uhuskic@sympatico.ca.

My intention is to include some of these suggestions and endorsements in a later edition of the book.

Thank you,

Uzeir Huskic
Toronto, Canada
May 30, 2008

Appendix

The Preamble and Chapter I of the Charter of the United Nations

The Charter of the United Nations was signed on June 25, 1945, in San Francisco, California, at the conclusion of the United Nations Conference on International Organization. It was enacted on October 24, 1945. The Statute of the International Court of Justice is an integral part of the Charter. The Charter consists of nineteen chapters and can be accessed at www.un.org .

The Preamble and Chapter I of the Charter of the United Nations follow:

PREAMBLE

WE THE PEOPLES OF THE UNITED NATIONS DETERMINED

- to save succeeding generations from the scourge of war, which twice in our lifetime has brought untold sorrow to mankind, and

- to reaffirm faith in fundamental human rights, in the dignity and worth of the human person, in the equal rights of men and women and of nations large and small, and

- to establish conditions under which justice and respect for the obligations arising from treaties and other sources of international law can be maintained, and

- to promote social progress and better standards of life in larger freedom,

And For These Ends

- to practice tolerance and live together in peace with one another as good neighbours, and

- to unite our strength to maintain international peace and security, and

- to ensure, by the acceptance of principles and the institution of methods, that armed force shall not be used, save in the common interest, and

- to employ international machinery for the promotion of the economic and social advancement of all peoples,

Have Resolved To Combine Our Efforts To Accomplish These Aims

Accordingly, our respective Governments, through representatives assembled in the city of San Francisco, who have exhibited their full powers found to be in good and due form, have agreed to the present Charter of the United Nations and do hereby establish an international organization to be known as the United Nations.

Chapter I

PURPOSES AND PRINCIPLES

Article 1

The Purposes Of The United Nations Are:

1. To maintain international peace and security, and to that end: to take effective collective measures for the prevention and removal of threats to the peace, and for the suppression of acts of aggression or other breaches of the peace, and to bring about by peaceful means, and in conformity with the principles of justice and international law, adjustment or settlement of international disputes or situations which might lead to a breach of the peace;

2. To develop friendly relations among nations based on respect for the principle of equal rights and self-determination of peoples, and to take other appropriate measures to strengthen universal peace;

3. To achieve international co-operation in solving international problems of an economic, social, cultural, or humanitarian character, and in promoting and encouraging respect for human rights and for fundamental freedoms for all without distinction as to race, sex, language, or religion; and

4. To be a centre for harmonizing the actions of nations in the attainment of these common ends.

Article 2

The Organization and its Members, in pursuit of the Purposes stated in Article 1, shall act in accordance with the following Principles.

1. The Organization is based on the principle of the sovereign equality of all its Members.

2. All Members, in order to ensure to all of them the rights and benefits resulting from membership, shall fulfill in good faith the obligations assumed by them in accordance with the present Charter.

3. All Members shall settle their international disputes by peaceful means in such a manner that international peace and security, and justice, are not endangered.

4. All Members shall refrain in their international relations from the threat or use of force against the territorial integrity or political independence of any state, or in any other manner inconsistent with the Purposes of the United Nations.

5. All Members shall give the United Nations every assistance in any action it takes in accordance with the present Charter, and shall refrain from giving assistance to any state against which the United Nations is taking preventive or enforcement action.

6. The Organization shall ensure that states which are not Members of the United Nations act in accordance with these Principles so far as may be necessary for the maintenance of international peace and security.

7. Nothing contained in the present Charter shall authorize the United Nations to intervene in matters which are essentially within the domestic jurisdiction of any state or shall require the Members to submit such matters to settlement under the present Charter; but this principle shall not prejudice the application of enforcement measures under Chapter VII.

References

Below you will find a list of books and other materials that I have used in the writing of this book. In addition I have listed information for many of the other books that have helped me to see the world as I see it now.

Aizenstat, A.J. Survival For All. New York: Billner & Rouse, Inc., 1985.

Ali, Rabia, and Lawrence Lifschultz. Why Bosnia? Stony Creek: The Pamphleteer's Press, 1993.

Barnet, Richard J. Roots of War. Markham, Ontario: Penguin Books, 1973.

Blackburn, Simon. Being Good. Oxford: Oxford University Press, 2001.

Braden, Gregg. The God Code. Carlsbad, California: Hay House, Inc., 2004.

Buckman, Robert. Can We Be Good Without God? Toronto: Penguin Books, 2000.

Chomsky, Noam. Hegemony or Survival. New York: Metropolitan Books, 2003.

Chopra, Deepak. Peace Is the Way. New York: Three Rivers Press, 2005.

Dyer, Gwynne. War. Toronto: Stoddart Publishing Co. Ltd., 1985.

Emmott. Bill. 20:21 Vision. New York: Farrar, Straus and Giroux, 2003.

Galtung, John, and Daisaku Ikeda. Choose Peace. London: Pluto Press, 1995.

Gorbachev, Mikhail S. The Coming Century of Peace. New York: Richardson & Steirman, 1986.

Goulding, Marrack. Peacemonger. London: John Murray Publications, 2002.

Harman, Willis. Global Mind Change. Indianapolis: Knowledge Systems, Inc. and the Institute for Noetic Sciences, 1988.

Harris, Sam. The End of Faith. New York: W.W. Norton & Company, Inc., 2005.

Hertsgaard, Mark. The Eagle's Shadow. New York: Farrar, Straus and Giroux, 2002.

Hitchens, Christopher. God Is Not Great. Toronto: McClelland & Stewart Ltd., 2007.

Izetbegovic, Alija Ali. Islam Between East and West. Indianapolis: American Trust Publications, 1989.

Kant, Immanuel. Groundwork of the Metaphysic of Morals. New York: Harper & Row, 1964.

Kurtz, Paul. Humanist Manifesto 2000. New York: Prometheus Books, 2000.

Lavine, T.Z. From Socrates to Sartre: The Philosophic Quest. New York: Bantam, 1984

Linden, Eugene. The Future in Plain Sight. New York: Penguin Group, 2002.

Munro, David. The Four Horsemen. Secaucus, New Jersey: Lyle Stuart, 1987.

Ohmae, Kenichi. The End of the Nation State. New York: The Free Press, 1995.

Russell, Bertrand. Authority and The Individual. London: Unwin Hyman Ltd., 1988.

Smoker, Barbara. Humanism. London: National Secular Society, 1984.

Templeton, Charles. Farewell to God. Toronto: McClelland & Stewart Ltd., 1999.

Ullman, Harlan. Unfinished Business. New York: Kensington Publishing Corp., 2003.

Vidal, Gore. Perpetual War for Perpetual Peace. New York, Thunder's Mouth Press, 2002.

Wallis, Jim. God's Politics. New York: HarperCollins, 2006.

Walzer, Michael. Just and Unjust Wars. Basic Books, 1992.

Watson-Watt, Sir Robert. Man's Means to His End. Toronto: McClelland & Stewart Ltd., 1961.

Wright, John W. The New York Times 2007 Almanac. New York: Penguin Books, 2006.

Zaehner, R.C. The Concise Encyclopedia of Living Faiths. Boston: Beacon Press, 1967.

Acknowledgments

Special thanks to Boba, my wife of thirty-four years, for an exciting life together and many deep discussions about life, justice, fairness, honesty, and interaction among people, without which I would be a different person.

Deep appreciation and thanks to my daughter, Belinda, for volunteering to read the manuscript and provide me with many valuable suggestions.

I would like to apologize especially to my wife Boba and to my daughter Belinda, son Ben, son-in-law Dave, nephew Salko, and grandchildren Shaheem, Shameen, and Isabelle for not being physically and mentally available to them for the last few months during my final work on this book.

I would also like to apologize to my relatives, friends, and colleagues for not being in touch with them as much as I would like to be since my retirement, due to work on the book.

Many thanks to iUniverse for valuable editing work and the opportunity to publish the book of my lifelong dreams in a relatively short amount of time.

In addition, I would like to acknowledge that the effort has been made to contact copyright holders and I would be pleased to hear from those that have not been contacted.

Uzeir Huskic
Toronto, May 30, 2008